GIRL GOES

MISSING

CLIVE E SMITH

S I Y A G R U V A

A series of novels for South African teens

First published 2003
Second impression 2006

© New Africa Books (Pty) Ltd
99 Garfield Road
Claremont 7700
South Africa

ISBN: 1-86928-346-5

Series editor: Robin Malan
Copy editor: Celia Fleming
Proof reader: Richard Rufus-Ellis
Text design and layout: Jenny Wheeldon
Cover design and layout: Orchard Publishing
Photographs: John Haigh

Origination: House of Colours

Printed and bound in the Republic of South Africa by
Shumani Printers

Chapter 1

The newspapers in Cape Town carried the headlines:

THREE MISSING CHILDREN IN THE WESTERN CAPE

PARENTS OF MISSING CHILD ANXIOUS

POLICE SEARCH FOR MISSING THREE

FOUR MISSING AFTER WEEKEND

Parents everywhere were growing more and more concerned for the safety of their children. Communities lashed out at the police in anger.

FIVE MISSING. POLICE HAVE NO CLUE

Many schools called PTSA meetings as the concern grew. Principals came out from behind their desks to talk to parents and to assure them they would do all in their power to stop their children from going missing!

Friday. Everyone was gathered at the Siyagruva Scene as usual, but something was different. No one was dancing, no one was listening to Raymondo. Instead, the Siyagruvers were gathered around the plastic table next to the cooldrink machine. Everyone had a sheet of newspaper in their hand. Concentrating. Extracting. Searching. They couldn't find a single clue that might explain the missing kids.

'This is such rubbish!' complained Shelley. 'All this writing, but they don't say anything!'

'Yeah. "Western Cape" – that could be anywhere!' said Thabiso.

'A girl has gone missing from our school ...' said Regan softly.

'What? And you're only telling us now! Man, that's right under our noses!' Thabiso shouted at Regan as he rammed his wheelchair into the plastic table.

'Sorry, I'm not even sure. We're not supposed to talk about it until all of the family know or have been informed. Don't be cross with me, the police don't want us to cause a panic,' said Regan with his head hanging so low they could hardly hear him.

Everyone was upset with him but they knew what he was going through and didn't want to add more pressure. He was their Siyagruva brother and at the Siyagruva Scene you didn't treat people badly. Besides, they had no idea what his relationship was with this girl. They felt for him, in spite of how curious they all were about the case of the missing kids.

Raymondo didn't feel like taking dance classes that afternoon. He wondered if his sister's daughter was safe. He licked his index finger and rubbed out a sticky orange cooldrink spot on the table, and said, 'I know nobody feels like dancing, but let's just do a warm-up or something. It'll get our minds off this thing ...'

He clapped his hands, but without his usual passion for his work. Thabiso half-heartedly wheeled himself towards the sound equipment. Dragging their feet, the others got up and started to move into a warm-up, heads hanging low, really wanting to question Regan some more. Emotionally, they all withdrew into their own headspace to think out this crisis. They warmed up for almost an hour without breaking a sweat.

Botes's telephone rang from somewhere under a pile of papers and files on his desk.

'*Ek is nie ... hier nie!*' A large voice came from behind a newspaper with the headlines:

POLICE HAVE NO CLUE
Five missing

The man behind the paper with his legs crossed on his desk next to a cup of cold coffee and a burger still in the clingwrap was none other than Detective Brandt Botes. He was a big-boned man, not fat, his face filled with tiny hairline scars from a mountain-climbing accident when he was young. He spoke with a deep voice, with his lips hardly moving.

He was known for his piercing blue eyes and his lack of humour – and his designer *velskoens*. Nobody knew where he came from. Nobody remembered him being in the army with anybody they knew.

He had been assigned to the case. After all, he was South Africa's finest. He was the one who solved the case of the missing three back in '92. He captured the notorious TV-killer. He caught the N2-hijack twins.

He was on lunch-break and didn't like the idea of being bothered by news reporters or anyone else. Behind him on the pinboard were the pictures of the victims and bits of file material stuck underneath each one. At this point in the investigation, he had to admit that he didn't have a clue.

'I always get my man!' he said, mumbling from behind his paper. *'Ek sal hom kry ...'*

And he would, too, he always did ... well, except for the Black Widow. She was hit by a taxi before he could arrest her for smuggling in Mandrax buttons from Malaysia.

Chapter 2

The Austin Cambridge A55 Mk II 1961 drove up to the school gate. Its two-tone, well-polished outside almost blinded the principal as he hurried toward the gate. Botes hooted impatiently, and the over-weight Mr Waybridge nervously headed towards him.

'I've been expecting you, Detective,' he

called out, out of breath, to the driver of the car.

'*Ja man, maak die hek oop, ek het nie heeldag tyd nie,*' Botes mumbled behind his hand.

Mr Waybridge opened the huge lock and chain on the gate with a key dangling from a string around his neck. No one was allowed in or out without his knowing about it. Waybridge was a kind man, with a small mouth and a small round pink chin like the rubber stopper you find on the front of roller-skates. He was a Sumo wrestler in a cheap suit. Not the strict type but the caring type, he loved education and always inspired his pupils to learn. He knew he would never catch the kidnappers, but he wanted to assure the parents that their kids would be safe in his school.

'Nice car.'

'This, *meneertjie*, is not just a car ...' Botes said in his deep no-nonsense voice.

'How old is it?' asked Waybridge in a friendly manner.

'Are you a mechanic or a principal?' Botes mumbled.

'Sorry?'

'Nothing. Are the parents here yet?'

'Yes, they're in my office ... this way.'

The parents of Nicole, the latest missing girl, were sitting in two chairs pushed together. They were holding hands. The mother had just stopped crying. You could tell by the parents' features that Nicole was a pretty girl.

'This is Detective Brandt Botes, he's in charge of the case,' Waybridge indicated with his fat arm.

'Is there any news yet?'

'No, ma'am, not at this time. I won't keep you very long, as I know this is a difficult time for you both.'

'Thank you,' the couple said together.

The mother started to cry again and the husband squeezed her hand.

'How far do you live from the school, and can you show me on the map here the route that Nicole used – uses – to get home?'

He unfolded a photocopied map-section from his inside pocket and laid it gently on her lap. Waybridge handed her a red koki.

The questioning started and the parents slowly came to trust Botes to find whoever had done this to them and to the community.

Waybridge found this a good time to wipe the sweat from his face and neck.

Botes got up and promised the parents that he was doing his best to track these criminals down. He told them that he, too, had a daughter. They smiled at him as Waybridge hurried to his feet to see Botes out. He waved at them to follow the detective out. They jumped up, almost embarrassed that they might have made the fat man get up yet again. He tried to shuffle past them, with no success. He hung back, and only managed to pass them as they got into their respective cars. He hurried to unlock the gate for them. As they drove off, he gave a friendly wave, but no one waved back. He smiled, anyway, and locked the gate safely.

Chapter 3

Shelley stayed apart from the rest of the group after a really hard workout. She was pleased that she did, but had no idea why she was feeling withdrawn like this.

When she got home, she went straight up to her room. She didn't even put any music on. She flung herself on to her bed and lay there, with her head hanging over one side of the bed and her feet over the other side, frowning, and with her eyes fixed on a single spot on the ceiling.

A corner of her mouth curled up and a smile appeared. The lines on her face smoothed out and her eyes narrowed, wickedly.

She had a plan!

'I'll take over the world ...' she threatened in a deep voice and turned on to her stomach. Staring at the Will Young poster on the wall, she said, 'Well, maybe not take over the world, but at the very least I'll ... plot my own kidnapping. Maybe my father will notice me then!'

She knew her father was the CEO of a big export-import company. ASDI or something. She thought about the man in the wedding photo on the mantelpiece in the living room. He still looked young, although he was much older now than in the picture. Shelley suspected he might be having an affair. Her mom had tried to convince her that he wasn't and that he worked such long hours only to give the two of them the things they needed and wanted. Shelley thought that her parents were only staying together for her sake.

'Let's see. I can't ask Bru, she's too honest, and she's sick of my plotting and planning ... I can't ask any of the other Siyagruvers either ... I need someone on the outside ... mmm ...'

She pushed the button. Her cellphone lit up ...

9 speed-dial, Regan. Calling!

'Hi, Regan, howzit goin', dollface?'

'Cool, who's this?'

'Shelley, duh!'

'Right. What do you want?'

'Ooh, crabby, aren't we?'

'It's jus' that I'm watching TV.'

'Sorry! I'll make it quick. Do you have Giempie's number?'

'What?'

'You heard me ...'

'Why do you want his number? He's a *skollie*, man!'

'I know, but a cute *skollie* ...'

'Are you bored again?' Regan shouted into the phone and cut her off, tired of her childishness.

9 speed-dial, Regan. Calling!

'Yes?'

'Me again ... I'm serious!'

'This guy robs people and he's been to jail, you know. I don't think a nice white girl like you must have anything to do with a *skorrie-morrie* like Giempie!'

'Just give me his number already!'

'Noooo! People say he only baths on his birthday ...'

'Are you jealous?'

'What, are you mad in your head? No!'

'So just give me his number!'

'No!'

'So, you *are* jealous, then.'

'No, why don't you just go and sit in your jacuzzi and leave me alone?'

'We don't have one. So you think I'm cute, huh?'

'Nooo, I mean yes, I mean no, *aaag* ... just don't call me again!'

9 speed-dial, Regan. Calling!

'What now? *Jislaaik*, woman, don't you ever give up?'

'Just give me the number, you sexy thing.'

'I'm not sexy ... I mean ... Okay, okay!'

Shelley took down the number.

'Thanks.'

'And don't say I didn't warn you!'

'Thanks, but you mustn't tell a soul about this conversation. I don't want anyone to know, specially not the rest of the sewing circle.'

'The what circle ...?'

'Just don't tell anybody, okay?'

'Fine, fine ... *Jislaaikit!*' he moaned and wondered what the hell he had just done. And then he promptly forgot about it and went back to the TV series he'd been watching earlier.

083 876 5432 Calling!

'Giempie, is that you?'

'Who want to know?'

'It's Shelley.'

'Who? My parole officer?'

'No, silly. I'm in Regan's dance group.'

'Which one is you?'

'The blonde one, duh!'

'The one with the *lekke*' ...'

'No, the white girl, the only white girl!'

'I'm *mos* saying so, the one with the *lekke*' ...'

'I need your help.'

'Well, just mak'it quick, this izza stolen phone, I don' want MTN to trace me, *djy wiet mos*, incognito!'

'Okay, sorry. Will you meet me on Mowbray station tomorrow at three?'

'Mak'it Rosebank station, I'm wanted in Mowbray.'

'Okay, see you there.'

Surprised at the business-like way Giempie handled the whole thing, she flipped over on to her back, grinning from ear to ear as her master plan unfolded.

At 3.03 p.m. the train squealed to a stop at Rosebank station. Two people got off, nobody got on. One of the two was Giempie. She waited for him, but he seemed to be talking to somebody else further along the platform. The train had already left and Giempie was still standing talking to some girl. The girl he was talking to was getting upset. Shelley suddenly realised what was happening and rushed to the rescue. She apologised to the confused girl and waved her on her way.

'Shelley, oh, it's you, I t'ought forra sec dat blondie was you. *Jislaaik*, I'm glad, 'cause you prettier dan her onetime, *ek sê!*'

'Thank you. Let's just go and sit in the little park over there.'

'Romantic, *nog.*'

'Giempie, stop it, I'm not into you.'

'Don't worry, you will be … soon-soon.'

'Whatever. Let's get down to business.'

Shelley laid out the plans for her kidnapping to Giempie, who was all ears.

Chapter 4

Shelley was lying on her back on her bed as usual. She thought she was dreaming about Brandon October – or, maybe, it was this year's Jacques ... Then she realised that she wasn't dreaming, she was thinking. Thinking quite deeply.

She thought of all the times her father had never made it to any of her school functions. She remembered the first time. She was in primary school – Grade 1. Her first day at school. Both parents were supposed to drop her off. Where was her dad? Not there. No, he had better things to do than be there for her on her first day of school. He was flying to Bali to go and buy fabrics for his business.

At that point she didn't even know what or where Bali was, but she knew it was more important than her going to school for the first time. In the car her mother apologised all the way to the school. Shelley was crying. Mom was crying. Both of them were crying. It was supposed to be a proud day for all three of the Gordons, but only two were there. The other had had to go to Bali.

'Bali!' Shelley shouted at the A2 poster of Oprah on the wall. 'What's Bali, Oprah? You must have been everywhere in the world ... Tell me about Bali. Are there millions of hotels filled with businessmen buying material?' She looked at Oprah upside down. 'Why did he go to Bali that day? I don't remember much about that day, but I remember crying a lot and wanting my daddy to hold my hand. Oprah, I wanted to feel like all the other smiley happy girls that walked in with both their parents. Even Millicent Bouje, who didn't have a dad 'cause he died – her uncle came – he looked like a dad. But where was my dad? I had an empty space for a dad. Oprah. Oprah?'

She frowned her words away and rolled on to her stomach. She pushed back with her hands and sat upright on her knees.

She yanked her diary out of the bedside drawer and opened it at the first page. She looked over the page to recall the memory of when ... yes, this was another time her dad had not been there for her. It was the time when she won an award for spelling in Grade 4.

The handwriting at the bottom of the next page she flipped to was untidy. That was in Grade 7, the day he .... She paged wildly through the diary, noting all the times she had been made to feel unhappy and embarrassed because her dad was never there.

He always upped her pocket money, gave her a cellphone long before anyone else had one. She had credit cards for all the fashion boutiques, she could stay up late and watch TV. She had all she needed in material things, and she loved it. But she never had her dad.

'I never had him, Oprah. Not once!'

She gazed at Oprah looking down at her with a beaming 'I love America' smile.

'Harpo? Yellehs?' she mouthed, trying to reverse her own name, struggling with the pronunciation. 'Hellish! That must be my life, hey? Hellish! No, not hellish, it's been pure *Hell* since the day I was born. Born without a dad!' she snarled at the beaming Oprah, who was quite unaware of her crisis. She reached for her cell.

3 speed-dial, Samantha. Calling!

She waited for Samantha's usual greeting. It came:

'Speak!'

'Hi, doll. Was your dad there for you on the first day of school? You know, did he go with you and your mother on the first day, like?'

'Shelley? What are you going on about?

Do you know that you're late for practice?'

'Man, I forgot. But did your dad, did he?'

'Yes, of course he did. Now, come on!'

'On my way ... I totally forgot ...' she said, embarrassed, and clicked the phone off.

'Maaaaa!' she shouted, pulling her bag from under her bed and pushing the diary into the back of the drawer at the same time.

'*Maaaaa!*' she called again, making it her mother's fault that she was late.

'What is it?' her mother asked, worried, bumping into Shelley as she sped out of her room.

'I'm going to be late for practice at Siyagruva, Ma!'

'Gosh, darling, I'm sorry. I was chatting to Vah-key outside. The neighbours have complained about our elm tree dropping leaves in their pool. Quite a fuss the old lady made,' she explained, bustling Shelley through the kitchen into the garage.

'Bloody Bali,' Shelley cursed under her breath.

'Darling!' exclaimed her mom. 'I know she's getting on in years, but there's no reason to be calling the old bag names, my love.'

'What? What are you going on about now, Ma? The elm ... Varkie? And what's this about a bag of leaves ...?'

Shelley dismissed her mother's chatter, thinking only about her own pain.

'Careful, Ma, you nearly reversed right into Varkie – and I wish you'd stop calling him "Vah-key". It's Afrikaans "Varkie".'

'You know, love, you should listen to me more, you are so distant these days, it feels as if your father and I have lost you ...'

'Lost me! *Gha!* We lost Dad when I was in Grade 1,' she moaned and threw herself against the seat.

'Silly girl, you're not still upset about that day, are you? Your father had a very important meeting in Bali that week.'

'*Ja*, whatever. Has he ever been there for me, like, for me ... for Shelley-bloody-Gordon! Ha! I'm a joke! "Hey, Shelley, where's your dad?", "Hey, Shelley, is your mom divorced?", "Hey, Shelley, is your mother a lesbian, then?" '

She pounded her fist into the passenger seat to punctuate each of her sentences.

'Shelley! You stop that right now, you hear. Nobody calls me a lesbian!'

Shelley's mom was quiet and thought for a while. When they stopped at a robot, she asked in a low voice, 'They don't really call me a lesbian, do they? I mean ... at your school?'

'No, Ma! They don't. I just used it for effect, but you're more worried about being called a lesbian than ... than about Dad not being there for me. For us. Don't you get it?'

'I do, my love, but if people are starting to call me a lesbian ... I'm talking to your father, wherever the hell he might be, tonight!'

'Drop the lesbian thing, Mother-Dear.'

'Well, he's just got to fly back from wherever he is tonight and be home by morning. This has got to stop!'

'Good luck, Ma. I hope he doesn't disappoint you! He's disappointed me for sixteen years and five months. Good luck!' Shelley shouted into the car as she got out before her mom had even pulled the handbrake up.

Chapter 5

Shelley ran in at the side entrance to the building and down the stairs. She bumped into someone, apologised and carried on running down.

'Shelley! Stop! It's me, Sam!'

Shelley reached the bottom of the stairs and looked round to see Samantha recovering from the mini-accident.

'Sam, sorry man, I was late, I didn't see you.'

'It's fine, but just stop. I want to talk to you before you go in.'

'Okay. But I'm already late.'

'It won't take a minute, okay?'

'Okay.'

'I was speaking to Regan. He's worried that you might be up to something and might need a sista to talk to. I know we haven't been that close but I want to be here if you want to talk, you know, even about sex ...'

Sam said this in a low voice in the echoing stairwell.

'Fine, thanks, I'll remember that when I feel the need to have sex. Thanks, Oprah, can we go now? I don't want to be late again – you know how Raymondo gets ...'

Shelley dropped a broad fake smile and walked quickly towards the entrance of the studio.

She was just inside the door when her cellphone rang. Fumbling through her togbag, she got to it just before it stopped ringing.

'Hello, Shelley speaking.'

'Shelley, it's Sam.'

'Sam! Please! Get a life!' She looked around, waiting for Samantha to come through the doorway to drop her another fake-smile-duh-move-on.

'Percy, I just want to be there for you, you know, like a friend, a sista, anything. Why are you being so mean about me wanting to help you?'

Sam moved in closer and took her by the elbow. Shelley pulled away.

'If I want your help, I'll ask for it. Besides, I don't want to fight with you, but there's nothing going on and I don't want to have sex with anybody.'

'I know you're upset now, but I'll phone you when you get home after the class so we can chat, okay?'

'Okay, friend! We'll *chat*!' Shelley said and shoved past her towards Raymondo who was about to clap his hands to get the class going.

During the warm-up, Sam moved Brunette out of the way so that she could be next to Shelley.

'Percy? Don't be mad with me, all I want to do is help and you're not letting me in ...'

When Shelley heard Samantha use that stupid nickname, she flipped.

'Samantha, if there's a problem *I* will ask

you to help *me.*' She stopped dead in her tracks and turned to face Sam. *'But there is no problem here! Do-you-under-stand-me?'*

Thabiso came wheeling over at full speed.

'You girls okay?'

'Fine!' the two girls chorused together, rolling their eyes so that Thabs wouldn't pry into their argument.

'Fine, let's carry on, Raymondo, from the top please?'

'Hey, Thabs, that's my line! Okay, class, from the top please,' Raymondo said.

The studio was filled with whispers the entire session, but no one actually said a word. They wanted to help the girls solve their problem but they had to give them a bit more time to sort it out themselves.

Thabiso kept an eye on what was going on, who was whispering with whom, who was trying to find out, who knew what was going on, who knew but wasn't telling, and who would like to tell even if they didn't know.

The class ended, with Thabiso still keeping an eye out. As they gathered in the changing area, he wheeled himself closer, pretending to be busy with a pile of CDs on his lap. He was close enough to hear but was not going to be drawn into anything with anybody. His sharp ears picked up only part of a conversation between Rashaad and Brunette. It was obviously all about the incident between Shelley and Sam. Feeling the tension in the air, he decided to leave things alone.

Outside the group split up. Shelley and Sam were waiting for their parents, Shelley for her mom and Sam for her dad. Standing about ten metres apart, they glanced at each other every few seconds.

Sam decided to phone Shelley – maybe it would make things a bit easier between them.

'Hi, girlfriend.'

'Hi, Sam.'

'Sorry 'bout today, I was just worried about you. Guess I went about things the wrong way, huh?'

'Yes, you did, Sam, and I'm sorry too – you know, for treating you that way,' said Shelley, looking at Sam looking at her. The two girls began to feel a bit silly. They laughed out loud and walked towards each other.

'Really, you must tell me if there is something that bothers you, please, Percy, okay?'

'Yes, fine Oprah, I will ...' said Shelley and pushed Samantha towards her dad's car, as it pulled up. 'Bye!'

'Bye!' Sam shouted from the window of her dad's car, with him also trying to get a wave in.

Chapter 6

It was 4 a.m. and Detective Botes was sitting in front of the TV screen in his flat. The room was dark and there was no sound coming from the television set. Botes was going over some of the tapes he'd got from security companies in the area of the school where the last girl, Nicole, had been kidnapped.

He was wearing his black-rimmed glasses, a white vest, boxers and socks with those funny suspender-goodies on. There was a half-eaten pizza in an open box on the coffee table with a 500 ml Coke resting snugly between two cushions beside him.

'*Gee my net iets, net 'n klein ietsie ...*' he mouthed softly at the remote control. 'Just something, any little thing, dammit!'

Suddenly he spotted a long sleek black car in one of the images. He jumped up and quickly cross-referenced it with the other tapes, and then checked with the map of the area to follow the car's movements towards the school.

The images on the security tapes were poor. The windows of the black car were tinted. He knew he didn't have much to work on, but at least it was a start.

'*Stadig maar seker, dalk nie vandag of môre nie, maar* ... any day now, sure as eggs is eggs.'

The next day the distorted image of the mysterious black car with the tinted windows appeared in all the newspapers.

Botes's assistant, Anthony Hawthorne, a *soutie* cop nicknamed 'Disco' – so called because of his flashy checked sports jackets – was a tall thin man with an almost violet tinge underneath his veiny skin. He looked sickly, as if he had some kind of disease that he refused to die from. Disco faxed all the small security companies, asking them about the mysterious black Citroën. Disco told them he could be contacted on his private cellphone number. Almost immediately he started getting calls about the car's movements. While he was on the cell he phoned Botes on the landline.

'Detective, perhaps you'd better get down here right away. I think we're on to something!' he said in his distinctive British accent.

'*Ek's nou daar, goeie werk, Disco*. Just give me ten minutes.'

'Right!'

Meanwhile more calls came in. Disco plotted the movement of the mysterious black car with little pins on the map on the wall behind his desk. It disappeared every now and again and then reappeared in areas where there were security cameras.

'How's it going, Disco?' Botes asked as he walked into the police station, taking his jacket off.

'Just lost them again, sir.'

'Mmm ...' grunted Botes, looking at Disco sticking his little pins in.

'We'll have an exact location by morning, sir. They've got to stop somewhere. For petrol, food, cigarettes, something.'

'*Ek hoop so.*'

'We can get an undercover team on to them by morning. It's been two days since their last kidnapping.'

'I hope we can catch them. They don't seem to have any sort of pattern. We don't know where or when they'll strike again, *dêm bliksems!*'

'I know, it's like pushing an elephant up stairs,' Disco nodded.

'*Waarvan praat jy nou, man? Bleddie souties wat nie Afrikaans kan praat nie.*'

'Sorry, sir?'

'*Ja, jy, jy moet regkom!* How long have you lived in South Africa?' Botes asked now that the phones were quiet.

'My whole life, sir.'

'*Nou hoekom klink jy soos* Remington Steele?'

'My parents, maybe. I've always talked like this.'

'*Blerrie soutie,*' Botes mumbled under his breath.

'Excuse me, sir? I didn't catch that.'

'*Nee, niks.*'

The Siyagruvers were lying in little heaps of breath-heaving sweat-bags. There was no moving them. Shelley looked towards the door to see if her mother had arrived to fetch her. She was exhausted.

Thabiso came wheeling over from behind the controls, dabbing his forehead with his handkerchief, singing one of his favourite Babyface songs. As he got closer, he maintained the melody but changed the words.

'... You guys are sooo sweet, and pathetic, I love you ... ooo ...'

Everybody got up and laughed at the Thabs-silliness and towelled themselves down so that they could get changed.

Shelley remained on her back, and grabbed Rashaad's leg. Up on one knee, he looked down, wanting to diss her but he saw the worry in her eyes. He saw the tears just below the surface. Before bending down to speak to her, he looked around to make sure that no one was going to come closer and try to interrupt them.

Rashaad knelt down next to her. She couldn't get the words out and stared deeply into his eyes. Rashaad could see the pain.

'It's your parents, isn't it?'

He recognised something in Shelley that he felt he knew.

'How did you know?' she whispered, looking around, to see if anybody was coming.

'You know what I've been through with my parents. I don't have to tell you. There was something odd about you when you came in earlier. I thought it was just because you were late, but I could see there was something the matter.'

'My father ...'

'Your father? Is he touching you, Shelley? I'll ...'

Rashaad almost jumped to his feet in anger.

'Shhh!'

She pulled him back, and settled herself with her head in his lap.

'Shhh, I don't want anybody to know. Well, I do want people to know, but I need to speak to one person first.'

She held him tight, not letting go so that she could look into his eyes.

'Why don't we get dressed and then you can tell me all about it, before your mom comes to get you.'

'Okay, but don't let on that you know anything. I told my mom, but I don't want her to know that the Siyagruvers know about our personal lives, like.'

'Don't worry, you don't even have to say anything else. It's obvious it's something to do with your dad. Is he ignoring you? Not enough time for you and you miss him and stuff ...?'

'Rashaad, you're so sensitive, a lot more than Samantha is. I can't even speak to her these days. She's got boys on her mind, you know ...'

'Don't we all!' he said with a nasal American twang. Shelley giggled.

'But seriously, I haven't seen my dad in weeks. You guys don't even know what my dad looks like. Hell, I don't even know what he looks like anymore.'

She sighed, as she put on her tracksuit.

'Do you think he's having an affair?'

'Nah, he's too fat and ugly. Too busy for that stuff, anyway.'

'Maybe you should try to get his attention, you know, do something he likes, or dislikes – I don't know, but do something!'

'Don't you worry, my little dancer-friend, don't you worry ...' she mumbled as they walked out of the Siyagruva Scene together.

Chapter 7

Brandt Botes stopped outside the UCT film unit. Campus Control rushed up to tell him that he couldn't park there without a disc. As the campus control officer's hand touched his elbow, Botes froze in his tracks. His head dropped and his detective hat cast a shadow over his face. Holding the box with the tapes close to him, he turned. The

Security loosened his grip on his elbow. Botes bent over, still not making eye contact with the guard, and dropped the box on the ground.

'*Luister hier, mannetjie ... as jy weer aan my raak ...*'

'Sorry, but you can't park here without a disc,' said the narrow-faced guard. He said this a hundred times every day.

The case had been a hard one and Botes didn't feel like talking. He took a deep breath.

'I am Detective Brandt Botes, please may I park here without a disc? Police business,' he said with a sigh.

'Detective, right! Everyone's a detective these days! Disc-holders only,' the guard said, half laughing, looking more like a prehistoric bird than when he first arrived.

Botes grabbed him by the shoulder and pulled out his badge-wallet.

'*Luister hier, meneertjie, dís my* disc! *Nou gaan speel met jou maatjies voor ek jou disnis klap!*'

'*Jammer, meneer. Kan ek die boks dra?*'

'*Mannetjie ... as ek jou ooit weer sien ...*' – he left the sentence unfinished – '*Hoor jy?*' growled the angry Botes. He brushed past the guard, and headed for the double doors at the top of the stairs.

'I'm looking for Brittany,' he said to the young student coming through another double door.

'She's in there,' he pointed over his shoulder.

Botes stood just inside the doors as they closed slowly behind him. The class suddenly quietened and the talking turned to whispers. He looked around the room to find Brittany. A head with the blondest and straightest hair you have ever seen. Eyes blue as the deepest blue-sky day. He spotted her. She turned as she felt someone staring at her from behind.

'Dad!'

He smiled for the first time in weeks. She rushed over to him. Unable to hug him with the box in his arms, she leaned over for a kiss on the cheek. Botes blushed.

'"Dad"?' he asked, bewildered.

'Sorry, *Pa, almal praat Engels hier.*'

'*Jy lyk pragtig. Hoe gaan dit met jou ma?*'

'*Sy's* okay, *Pa. Sy't toe daai* job *gekry.*'

'*Watter een?*'

'*Die van* Staff Secretary *vir daai* Mark Shuttleworth-Campaign-Against-World-

Hunger *of so iets.'*

'En die Beetle*?'*

'Nee, sy loop nog lekker. Dankie, Pa, dit was die beste verjaarsdagsgeskenk ooit. Maar wat soek Pa hier en wat's in die boks?'

'Video tapes *van 'n* case *wat ek aan werk.'*

'Die kidnappings*? Ek het in die koerant gelees.'*

'Ek het die tapes *gemerk met 'n* koki *en genommer. Ek wil hê jy moet al die* frames *met die swart kar in vir my op een* tape *sit, asseblief.'*

'Hoeveel tapes *is daar?'*

'So tien of twaalf.'

'Vir Pa ... enigiets!' and she smiled broadly, proud that she could do something to help him for a change.

Botes looked coy as she saw him out. He felt a little shy that he had to ask his baby for help. It would make things easier to have all the sightings of the black car on one tape.

Late that evening Brittany phoned him with the news that the tape was ready. He asked if she could enlarge the best picture to make out at least something of the licence-plate number. She called back later to confirm that she'd managed that. He hung up the phone and drove to the lab to collect the box of videos.

Back home he studied the new tape and wrote down all the number-plate combinations he could come up with.

He leant over the mess on his couch to reach the phone.

'Disco, hou jouself gereed, mannetjie. Ek dink die bom gaan môre bars!'

Not waiting for the half-asleep Disco to respond to being woken up to news of some bomb or other, he hung up. Relieved.

Chapter 8

S helley called her mom during her break.

2 speed-dial, Mom. Calling!

'Ma, can you pick me up a bit later today? We're going swimming at the gym after school. Maybe an hour later?'

'Okay, see you then.'

'Bye.'

16 speed-dial, Giempie. Calling!

'Hello?'

'Giempie?'

'Ja, who want to know?'

'It's Shelley ...'

'Who, my parole officer?'

'No, stupid, Shelley!'

'Sorry, girl.'

'Are you ready for this afternoon? Quarter-past-three, remember. I'll be walking from school.'

'*Ja, man*, I'm not stupit.'

'I don't want you to mess this up. Have you got the car already?'

'*Ja, man*. Have you got the rest of the money?'

'Yes, I'll give it to you in the car.'

'*Lekke*', see you later. I can't talk for long ...'

'I know, incognito ...'

'*Djy's wee*' cute *va'dag, nè!*'

'Just be on time.'

'Okay-okay, *baai, jou lekke' ding.*'

Giempie asked his friend Walter if he could use his car for a job. He promised he'd change the number plates. Walter waited until Giempie taped the fake plates on to the black Cortina with double-sided tape. As Walter handed the keys over, he asked – as he had done many times before:

'Cut me in?'

'*Wa', is djy mal? Djy's dan 'n kê'kbroe'!*'

'*Ek wil net 'n cut hê, ek willie wiet waar'ie geld vandaan kom nie, broe'-*Giempie. Where the money come from is not my business.'

'*Net om'at my ma en jou ma saam kê'k toe ga'n* meanie *djy kan 'n cut kry nie.* You shouldn' mix church and business.'

'No cut, no car,' Walter said, and hugged the keys to his chest.

'*Twee honnit rand*, not a cent more. *Djy's vannie duiwel af!*' Giempie exclaimed, looking left, then right. '*Wat van honnit-en-vyftig?*'

'Deal!' Walter said, and handed him the keys.

'*Blerrie kê'kbroe's is oekma' net soe skelm!*' Giempie mumbled when he was out of earshot, and got into the car.

Shelley's cellphone rang. She glanced at the screen. What did Samantha want *now*?

'Yes, Sam, what do you want?'

'Don't you give me grief, girl. Now I definitely wanna know what's going on.'

'What d'you mean?'

'Look, Rashaad's not the most streetwise guy in the world, but even he thinks you're up to something. I want to know what.'

'All right,' sighed Shelley, 'but you have to swear you won't try to stop me.'

'So what's the point of knowing, then? Don't answer that. Just tell me.'

Shelley told Samantha what was going on.

'Jeez, girl, I'm impressed! That'll make your dad *skrik* all right ... but ...' and Samantha's voice faltered a little.

'But ... what?' demanded Shelley.

'Isn't it, like, a bit dangerous? And what if your folks freak and call the police and stuff like that?'

'Well, that's the whole point, sista! Look, he's got to be taught a lesson! And if that means calling out the whole SANDF, then cool! Look, Sam, thanks for phoning, but

I've gotta go. Places to be, things to do, y'know. Bye.'

Samantha looked at the lifeless phone in her hand, frowned, and shrugged her shoulders.

'Well, I tried.'

Giempie stopped two streets down to pick up his wheelman. Balla was waiting for him at the gate of his house. They quickly painted a thick white line on the sides of the car – called The Black Jemima – with tennis-shoe whitening.

'Jus' for good luck,' laughed Giempie. 'And so nobody thinks it's the car they think it is, *djy wiet*! *Klim in*, let's go!'

Balla took the wheel. Once in the car, they went over the plan two or three times. Balla wasn't stupid, but he needed this to go well. His mother was sick and not working anymore, and there was no one to pay for him to study art. He didn't know who his father was and he didn't think his mother did either. All he wanted to do was get out of the ghetto. Balla was a really good mural artist and wanted to make something of his life. Giempie said that was why he had cut Balla in.

Damn! There was *Uptown Girl* again. Shelley fished out her cellphone.

'Sam, what do you want? I'm right in the middle of the biggest adventure of my life and you keep *hakking* me!'

'Look, lady, you do what you want, you know what I mean? But I still want to ask if it's really okay.'

'If *what's* okay?'

'I mean, getting everyone all steamed up. You know how upset your ma will get ...'

'*Ja*, I do know that, and I'm sorry, but ...'

'And how will we know if you're okay? We worry about you, too, you know.'

'I know you do. And thanks. But don't.'

'I don't want to use heavy words, like "Aren't you being a bit irresponsible?" ...'

'Well, then don't. Look, Sam, I've just got to go. It's time. If I go on talking to you, it'll spoil everything. Like, I'm too busy on my cell to be kidnapped! I tell you what. I promise if anything bad happens, I'll phone you. If you don't hear from me, you know everything's okay. Okay? Bye.'

Samantha looked glumly at her phone. She knew she wouldn't switch it off for one second until all this was over.

The Black Jemima took the corner slowly. Balla checked for cops and cameras, and Giempie looked out of the window to see if he could spot Shelley. He would know her by her pink silk scarf. There she was! Just at the corner of the school grounds, heading down the side road. Balla turned off the music in the car. They approached slowly. The gap: 200 m. They hung back and moved even more slowly. Balla gestured Giempie to roll up his window.

Suddenly there was a car coming towards them from the other direction. They almost stopped. It turned into the road where Shelley was walking. The car sped up to her, then braked violently, the back door opened, and hands grabbed her and pulled her on to the back seat. The door slammed. The car screeched into action, and roared off.

'*Haai!*' Giempie shouted, rolling down his window.

'*En nou?*' Balla asked, shocked.

The two stared at each other with pale faces. Shocked at what they'd just seen, without thinking, they sped after their money.

The kidnappers became aware of the car following closely behind and they knew that there was no way they'd be able to pull away from The Black Jemima.

'Dump de girl!' the masked driver said in a heavy accent.

'No way, this is a good one!' said the one holding Shelley in a tight grip.

'Come on, man, just throw her out at the next corner!'

'Fine, your loss ...' he said and loosened his grip on Shelley a bit, ready to throw her out at the next corner.

Luckily for Shelley, they couldn't run the next robot. Instead, the car mounted the pavement, and the big guy in the back heaved Shelley out, the car drove through the garden of the corner property, and then sped off.

'*Gryp haa'!*' shouted Balla, driving up to her.

Giempie opened the back door, jumped out and grabbed Shelley. Relieved, she jumped into the car willingly.

'Jeesh, am I glad to see you!'

'What de hell was going on wit dose guys stealing our bait?'

'Those must be the real kidnappers!' said Shelley, gasping to get her breath back. 'Am I glad you guys came! I was almost dead.'

Balla made a U-turn – and drove slap-bang into a fleet of police vans and cars. He drove straight through them. Tyres screeched and the police turned their vehicles around and followed The Black Jemima. The car in front had Botes and Disco in it. Disco was driving. Botes was cursing.

At first it looked as if they'd never get away, but Shelley knew that part of Rondebosch-Claremont well. The Black Jemima needed no introduction to the tight corners. They managed to lose the cops before the helicopter came to help them in the search. They hit the freeway into town and through to Green Point where Shelley's parents had a small flat they never used except when family from London came to visit (the ones they didn't like).

After the whole thing was over, the Gordons' gardener Varkie had a story to tell:

I was sitting there in Mr and Mrs Gordon's flat in Green Point. I heard the rumble of the car engine outside the window as the lights filled the room. I came out. It was them. Shelley was first, with the two scruffy guys behind her.

'Thanks, Varkie. Sorry we took so long,' she said to me in a sweet voice.

'My pleasure, Miss Shelley,' I said, keeping my head low.

'Now remember, don't tell my mother anything. And the flat keys that you "borrowed" from home to have the new ones cut for me to use – hang them back up in the kitchen behind the door at home.'

'Yes, Miss Shelley. I left the new keys I had cut here in this kitchen next to the kettle for you.'

'Thanks, Varkie! And stop calling me "Miss Shelley" – just call me "Shelley",' she said and led the other guys into the lounge and turned the lights on.

'I must go now, Miss Shelley, er, Shelley, or the missus will think I'm out jolling with the other gardeners in the street. I don't want to lose my job,' I said, heading for the door.

'Don't worry, man, Ma will never fire you, she loves you.'

Somehow that made me feel good about losing my job when the missus found out I was involved in this kidnapping thing.

'Can we stay here till after the six o'clock news? I want it to be safe before we leave,' Balla said.

'Sure. What's your name?'

'Par'n my manners, dis is my partner, Balla,' Giempie said. Shelley looked at Balla for a long time, sort of studying him. His scruffy hair and how it hung in his eyes all the time. His wide cheekbones, almost Mexican-looking, with smooth dark skin and deep dark eyes. His chest was wide and his shoulders looked like those of a boxer.

'Are you one?'

'One what?'

'A boxer?'

'I'm a artist, I paint murals ...'

'Mmm ... I can see,' she lied.

'Where's the rest of the money?' Giempie cut their conversation short.

'Oh, sorry, here,' she said, pulling the money out of her bra and giving it to Balla. From the other side of the table Giempie grabbed it and then divided it quickly into three piles.

'One for you, one for me ... and one for that *skelm-kê'kbroe*', Walter.'

Later, on the six o'clock news, there was a short report about the kidnapping. The car was described as black and white. The licence plate was wrong, and there was some confusion about whether it was a Cortina or a Citroën.

Before Giempie and Balla left, they washed the whitening off the sides of the car and put the original plates back on The Black Jemima.

Chapter 9

After Giempie and Balla left, just after dark, Shelley felt a great sense of empowerment.

She put the TV on the small coffee table and slid underneath a granny blanket with a big bag of chips. She was smiling from ear to ear. She felt as if this was her moment, her fifteen minutes of fame. She jotted down in her diary: 'GLORY DAYS'.

But it didn't last very long. She soon realised that she was cut off from the rest of the world. She couldn't answer her phone when it rang.

She checked to see if there were any text messages. There were SMSes from Sam, saying things like:

'Dont do it PerC'

and

'I h8 U when U 4get Ur frenz We luv U'

Then she listened to the voice messages. There was a long one, with her mother crying in the background and her dad saying that he had the army looking for her, and that he loved her very much.

After every voicemail message, she felt more and more loved, more and more missed. Like a spoilt brat. She hadn't ever realised before how much her dad really loved her. She listened to his messages over and over. Her eyes were puffy from crying. Suddenly she giggled, as she realised how important it was to have a waterproof phone.

Getting a lot colder, she pulled another granny blanky over her. She was shaking. She wished that she could speak to Rashaad again. She was even missing Sam. And her mom. Most of all, she wanted to speak to her dad. She wanted to tell him she loved him too. But he had to learn.

'He has to learn that things will be taken away from you if you don't love them the way you're supposed to.'

Suddenly she shouted into the cellphone.

'*Dad!* Yes, that's right, Daddy! You notice me now, don't you? ... Now that I'm gone ... Missing me? Missing me, aren't you, Mr Gordon?' she said sarcastically, pulling an ugly face.

Then suddenly his face appeared on the TV and she shrieked.

She got all tangled in the granny blankies as she tried to get to the TV to turn the volume up so that she could hear him. Her mother was folded under his arm. Sobbing. His eyes were red and watery.

'Shelley ... we love you very much, your mother and I ... and your friends. I just want to appeal to the kidnappers not to hurt her.

She's all we have. Our only ... ' – and here he sobbed but quickly brought himself under control – '... our only daughter. I'll pay any amount, just bring her back to us ... safe.'

The words rolled off his lips as if he was dealing with rich clients from China.

Shelley cried.

'Dad ... ?'

'Mr Gordon,' the reporter continued, 'has offered a large reward for any information leading to the capture of the kidnappers. Members of the public can contact Detective Brandt Botes of the Mowbray Police Station if they have any information concerning this case. This is Gavin Gavinson, SABC, Cape Town.'

The camera panned backwards to bring their house into the frame. Shelley cried even more, seeing her parents standing on the lawn of their big house. Now empty. Without her. Her bedroom light wasn't even on.

The last shots of the insert showed the Siyagruvers gathered on the lawn. They were all there, crying, expressing concern, saying they loved her, hoping that she would be returned safely.

Shelley wanted to pick up the phone and tell them that she was okay, but she couldn't. Mr Gordon had to learn a lesson.

'It hurts, but it's got to be done,' she said to herself.

With her eyes welling up with tears, she put the TV off, and fell asleep.

She woke up cold and lonely, but she had a plan. She was going to see this hotshot detective Botes at the Mowbray Police Station.

'Morning, I'm looking for Detective Botes,' she told a female cop at the front desk.

'He's over there,' she pointed, squinting her eyes at how familiar Shelley looked.

'Detective Botes?'

'Shelley Gordon?' he said, recognising her instantly from the profile on the wall behind him.

'Yes ...'

'Are you okay?' he asked, rushing over to her and wrapping her in his jacket. 'Here. Sit.'

'Thanks ...'

'Disco! *Koffie!*' Botes shouted at the

preoccupied Disco, hunched over the photocopy machine.

'Coming right up, sir,' he answered, not knowing who it was for.

Shelley was so nervous that she started crying. She had never been inside a police station before.

'Calm down, please, Ms Gordon. I assume that you have escaped. That's good. Did they harm you in any way?'

Shelley shook her head from side to side, wiping her eyes and her runny nose with Botes's coat.

'Disco!' he shouted again. Then, to Shelley, he said, 'I'll call your parents right away. Don't worry, you're safe now. You look so much like my own little girl. We were all worried sick about you – me and your parents, I mean.'

'Yes, sir?' Disco muttered, carrying the cup of coffee.

'Shelley Gordon, my assistant, Detective Hawthorne,' Botes introduced them, quite shocking the unsuspecting Disco.

'Sir!' Disco exclaimed.

'Ja, man, bel haar ouers!'

'On the double, sir.'

'Okay, so do you want to start telling me about the kidnappers? Your parents will be along in a few minutes.'

Shelley described the two kidnappers in great detail. She even amazed herself that she could remember so much of that short time in the back of their car.

Botes got in a sketch artist, and within the hour the two identikits were all over the news. Botes knew he'd get them now, he had all he needed. Car, registration numbers, good descriptions. 'In the bag, *boeta*!'

Shelley told Botes that Giempie and Balla had rescued her and that they deserved the reward money her dad had put up. She conveniently left out the fact that she had plotted her own kidnapping. No one needed to know that, and everybody would be happier not knowing, she thought.

Mr and Mrs Gordon were there to pick her up and she was reunited with her parents.

Botes leaned back in his old detective chair and locked his hands behind his head. He looked at the happy scene in front of him. And he thought of his own daughter. Was that a hint of a tear in his eye?

With Shelley safely back in his arms,

Shelley's father realised that he had been so busy making money that he had lost touch with his daughter.

'I understand now what I've missed out on,' he told Shelley. 'I had no idea how much I loved you until twenty-four hours ago.'

Shelley snuggled into his embracing arms.

'I think he's got the message ...' – she smiled to herself, happily satisfied with how well her plan had worked out – '... though I do admit I should maybe have done it some other way.'

Mrs Gordon drove them directly to the Siyagruva Scene, where all her friends were waiting to surround her with love and kisses and hugs and hundreds of questions. Apart from Samantha, none of them had any idea that Shelley had arranged her own kidnapping, which nearly went horribly wrong. So, they were just excited to have her back.

'What was it like?'

'Were you terrified out of your mind?'

'Did your kidnappers wear masks and things?'

'Why did the TV say you were wearing a pink silk scarf to school?'

'What's it like to be on television news?'

'How come *ou* Giempie got mixed up in it all?'

Shelley smiled all the time, and enjoyed answering the questions just as far as she wanted to.

Samantha pulled her aside for a moment, so that the others couldn't overhear, and said to her, 'I think what you did to your parents – and to us – really sucks. More important, I can't believe you never answered any of my messages! I'm never going to give you advice again. And I'm never going to phone you again, ever!'

Shelley pulled a face and stuck out the tip of her tongue to Sam, and said, 'Promise?' Samantha just moved off.

Rashaad leaned in close and said softly, 'It looks as if things are fine between you and your dad, hey?'

'*Ja*, it looks like it. But maybe in future I must just be more open and straight with my folks. It'll maybe cause less hassle, and probably work out better, anyhow. We'll see.'

She squeezed Rashaad's hand.

Shelley had a moment to herself. 'The

snag is,' she thought, 'this isn't going to stay a secret forever – something'll leak out some time. Sam has never been able to keep a secret! And then I'll have to deal with it with my parents. Maybe I should do that now, before it gets too difficult – and while my dad's still listening to me!'

The girl who had gone missing was home.

SIYAGRUVA

A series of novels for South African teens

BOY IN DA CITY

RUSLEEN MALBUSCH

The Siyagruvers have never had to handle anything as tricky as this! What do you do with a refugee boy who has no one to look after him and nowhere to go? Everyone has to pull together and help young Equiano.

'What's wrong with us that we can't all be welcoming and caring towards African foreigners? Why do people call them amakwerekwere?'
A reader

SIYAGRUVA

A series of novels for South African teens

DANCE IDOLS

ANNE SCHLEBUSCH

A nationwide competition to find some young dance idols! Who's going to enter, who's going to pull out, and why? And who's the least likely person in the Siyagruva Scene to win it? There are surprises all along the way in this Siyagruva story.

'It was just as exciting as watching the Idols on TV – I really wanted my favourite to win!'
A reader